For my daughter Adelaide,

who taught me where the stars live.

- G. T.

For my dad,

who taught me no question is too silly.

- K.C.

For further information, contact:
Tumblehome, Inc.
201 Newbury St, Suite 201
Boston, MA 02116
https://tumblehomebooks.org/

Library of Congress Control Number: 2020931754
ISBN 13: 978-1-943431-54-0
ISBN 10: 1-943431-54-X

Grant , Dr. Tremblay and Coppens, Katie
What Do Black Holes Eat For Dinner /
Dr. Grant Tremblay and Katie Coppens — 1st ed

Black hole (cover) image credit:
Niko Maisuradze & Dr. Grant Tremblay

Design: Yu-Yi Ling

Printed in Taiwan
10 9 8 7 6 5 4 3 2 1

TUMBLEHOME

What Do
Black Holes
Eat For Dinner?

And other silly, *yet totally smart,* questions about space

Dr. Grant Tremblay & Katie Coppens

T he most important thing to understand about space is how absolutely enormous it is. When you look at our Universe, there is endless possibility. It is the willingness to be curious and ask questions that has propelled humans' scientific understanding forward. And it is *your* willingness to ask questions that will propel *your* scientific understanding forward.

> Seriously? I can ask anything?

Anything. My guess is that your questions will lead to answers that surprise you, possibly even shock you, and definitely open up your thinking to more and more questions. I can't promise all of the answers to your questions are known, but I will answer them with the most accurate thinking that we have at the time that this book is published.

Let's see where your questions take us!

> Okay, here I go. What do black holes eat for dinner?

Great question. I like the way your mind thinks! But, to answer your question, we first have to understand a bit about black holes. You know your parents' vacuum cleaner? That big scary loud thing that roams the house devouring *everything* in its path? Well, that's *not* what a black hole is like. You may have been told that black holes suck in anything that dares to come near them, but it's just not true. Black holes don't "suck." They're nothing more than a mass. A very large mass, mind you, but just a mass nonetheless.

Well, you may be asking yourself, what is a mass? "Mass" is, basically, a measure of how much "stuff" is in something. As you grow bigger, your mass will increase. A big boulder has more mass than a small pebble. You might have guessed that mass sounds like the same thing as *weight*. Mass is a measure of the amount of material within an object, and weight is a measure of the force that gravity exerts on that object. This is why, if you went into deep space, your *weight* would effectively go to zero, but your mass would remain the same.

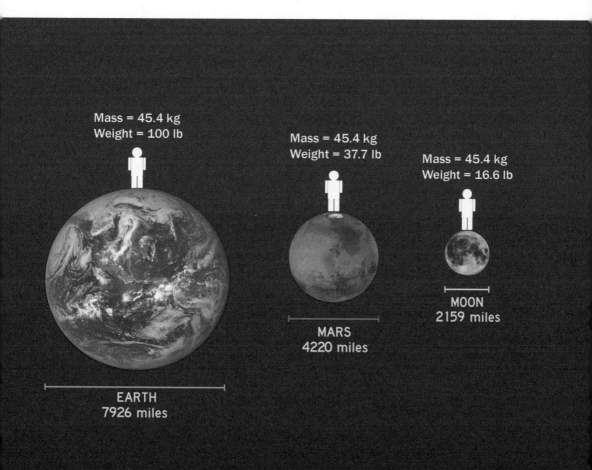

Anyway, to give you a sense of the size of the mass of a black hole, let's compare it to something we can picture, the nearest star to us — the Sun. If you were to replace the Sun with a black hole of equal mass, *nothing would change* with the orbit of the planets around it, including Earth. They would all keep on moving in exactly the same way they did when the Sun was there.

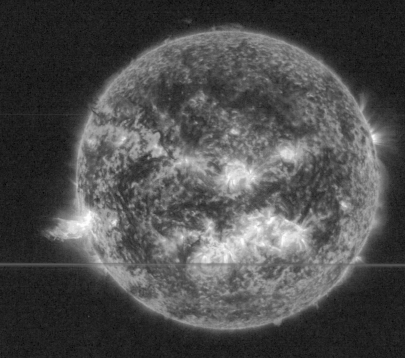

The Sun is 864,000 miles in diameter and has a surface temperature of 10,000 degrees Fahrenheit.
Credit: NASA

Of course, I don't want you wishing we were orbiting a black hole right now. First of all, if you were, you wouldn't be reading this. You see, black holes don't emit light like stars do. Our Sun is a star. Without the Sun's light and energy fueling all life on Earth, species couldn't survive, and without light Earth would literally and figuratively look very different.

Speaking of the way things look, let's picture a black hole. Do you literally picture a dark, black hole? Well, instead picture *blindingly* bright, white light. I know I just said black holes don't emit light. You'd only see this blindingly bright, white light in *the fraction of a second* before you were *vaporized*. That's right, if you were actually close to a massive black hole that was "accreting" (gobbling up gas), you wouldn't see a dark void of nothingness, but rather the incredibly intense radiation field given off by that infalling gas in its death spiral toward the "event horizon," which you can think of as a black hole's edge. As the gas falls inward, it collapses into a spinning vortex that, due to friction, superheats to millions of degrees. Gas that hot is also incredibly, blindingly bright, giving off a radiation field that would *fry* you very, very quickly.

If the black hole at the center of our galaxy were a bit more massive and consuming more gas than it is currently (that is, if it turned into a *quasar*), then there would be *no life on Earth!* Yes, the radiation would be so intense that, even though the black hole at the center of our galaxy is 26,000 light years (or 153 *peta*miles ... that's 152,844,000,000,000,000 *miles*) away, the radiation it would put out would be capable of killing everything on ... uhhh ... this series of questions is getting pretty grim. Again, you *really* don't need to worry about this. It's not gonna happen.

What is a quasar?

A "quasar" is a supermassive black hole that is eating a LOT for dinner! In consuming this all-you-can-eat buffet, the area surrounding the black hole becomes so bright that it outshines the ENTIRE GALAXY that it resides within. We call such an object a quasar.

Now, how large do you imagine a black hole to be? The size of a house? A planet? An entire solar system? Yes, yes, and yes. Black holes can grow to be larger than 10 billion times the size of our Sun. Imagine that! But black holes don't have to be massive. A black hole can have the mass of, say, a *mouse!*

Wait, a *mouse*?!

Schwarzschild diameter of a 10⁹ M$_\odot$ BH
———— ~40 AU ————

Credit: N. Maisuradze & G. Tremblay

A black hole is — you guessed it — very black, and therefore impossible to see directly. BUT, you CAN see the incredibly bright light emitted by matter that falls into the black hole, and you can even see the warping of space itself by the immense gravity of the black hole. In other words, you can see the effects that the black hole has on its surroundings, even if you can't see the black hole itself. The above artists' rendering is an example of what a supermassive black hole might actually look like if you could ever approach one (trust us, you wouldn't want to).
Credit: N. Maisuradze & G. Tremblay

You see, a black hole isn't called a black hole because of its size (although *it certainly can be enormous!*), but because it is extremely, extremely *dense*. "Density" is a measure of how much mass is contained within a certain "volume," or region of space. Something with higher density has more mass crammed into the same volume of space. There is much more mass in one cubic inch of rock, for example, than in one cubic inch of air. Imagine, say, the pillow on your bed. It's really easy to lift, right? Now imagine that your pillow were the same size, but made of solid rock. You probably wouldn't be able to lift it. This is because, being made of rock, there would be far more mass crammed into the same volume, relative to your actual pillow, which is stuffed with feathers or cotton.

This pillow and rock have about the same volume, but very different densities. Just think, when someone says their pillow is as hard as a rock, it actually could be that hard if the pillow had enough density.

Trust me, I promise there's a point to all of this.

Earth, thankfully, is not a black hole. But we could theoretically *make it* a black hole by squeezing it down to the size of a pea. All that cramming would make Earth super, super dense. Imagine cramming the entire mass of Earth, all 6,000,000,000,000,000,000,00 0,000,000 *kilograms* of it, into the size of a green pea. If we did that, the "escape velocity" from this now-smaller Earth would increase. Escape velocity is the speed an object must attain in order to completely escape the gravitational pull of another object. The escape velocity from, say, a cereal bowl, or your body, is extremely low.

Before we crushed Earth down to the size of a pea, the escape velocity of Earth was about 7 miles per second, or about 25,000 miles per hour. That's how fast a rocket has to get going to escape Earth's gravity and head off, say, to Mars.

But *after* we cram its mass into the volume of a

pea, the escape velocity from the surface of this... ahem, pea-sized world... *would be greater than the speed of light!*

Imagine Earth's mass crammed into the volume of a pea?

We're almost certain that the speed of light is the fastest possible velocity attainable by any matter in the Universe. This is because *accelerating* (speeding up) any object with any nonzero mass to the speed of light would require an infinite amount of energy. Did I lose you? Sorry. To put it simply, if some piece of mass has an escape velocity greater than the speed of light, *nothing can ever escape its gravitational pull,* not even light itself!

When this condition is met, the incredibly massive, incredibly dense object, like our pea-sized Earth, is shrouded in a purely mathematical boundary we call the "event horizon." Crossing this boundary means you would become

What's an event horizon?

An event horizon is the zone around a black hole in which light can no longer be given off.

causally disconnected from the rest of spacetime. So, there's that to think about. Let's be glad we're not on a compressed pea-sized Earth.

Wait, thinking about peas reminds me of something: what was your original question?

What's causally disconnected?

Causally disconnected means you are no longer part of the observable universe. Yep.

Um, my question was what do black holes eat for dinner?

Why, *everything!* Yep, all of that lead-up to that one answer — *everything!* Black holes may not roam like a vacuum, but they do shred stars apart and consume them whole. Giant clouds of gas fall toward black holes. As they get close, they pancake into a spinning vortex of superheated plasma that eventually falls into the event

What is plasma?

Plasma is the fourth state of matter (after liquid, solid, and gas). Plasma is an ionized gas. Typically electrons are in the nucleus, but the electrons in plasma move around more freely. It's like in an incredibly hot SOUP of electrons, protons, and neutrons. In a way, black holes eat really hot soup for dinner.

horizon. Now, do black holes eat pizza? Chicken nuggets? Peas (very funny...)? That has never been observed, but the answer cannot be a no. You see, if, say, Earth were to ever fall into the event horizon of a black hole*, its dinner would be pretty much like yours — chicken nuggets, with a side of PLANET.

*Again, *please* don't worry. This won't actually happen.

Um...I saw that little asterisk that said "*Don't worry, this won't actually happen." How do I know that Earth won't be "eaten" by a black hole?

I can't say this enough... The thing to remember is that space is really, *really, really* big. Impossibly, indescribably enormous. The chances of us ever coming even *close* to a black hole that could cause us any harm is just ridiculously, ridiculously low. I feel 100% confident that you can take black holes off of your worry list.

Okay, so I get that I shouldn't worry about Earth being "eaten" by a black hole. How about this? Can galaxies crash into each other?

This also does not belong on your list of things to worry about (I'm assuming you have a list of things you worry about based on your last two questions.) Just so you know, astrophobia is a real thing — it's a fear of everything involving space, like stars, aliens, etc. If you do have astrophobia, this probably isn't the best book for you.

It's totally normal to have *some* fears in life (like for some it's public speaking or heights), but I hope I can ease your space fears by reminding you again how absolutely enormous all of space is and how really, really small Earth is compared to it. To give a sense, Earth is one tiny little planet amongst over a hundred billion stars and planets in our one galaxy. Remember I told you that the Universe is crazy, super, enormously large. Our galaxy, the Milky Way, is just one of two trillion galaxies (yep, one of 2,000,000,000,000 galaxies).

Having said that, here I go… galaxies collide with one another *all the time*. This happened more frequently in the past, serving as a major driver of the growth of galaxies through cosmic time. Among the most energetic events in the Universe, these so-called "galaxy mergers" occur when two galaxies slowly wander too closely to one another. Their mutual gravity takes over, pulling them even closer together, until they finally collide.

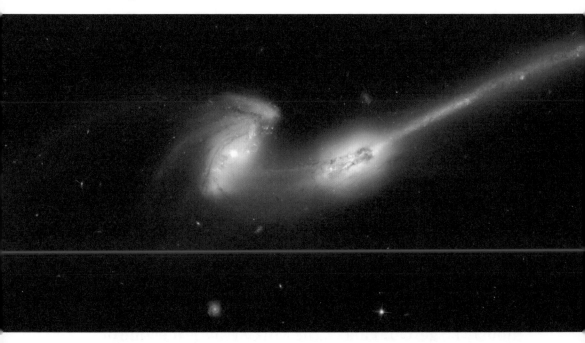

A Hubble Space Telescope image of the "Mice" Galaxies. Also known as NGC 4676, these are two galaxies that have passed close to one another and are in the process of "merging", or crashing into one another. Credit: NASA, H. Ford (JHU), G. Illingworth (UCSC/LO), M.Clampin (STScI), G. Hartig (STScI), the ACS Science Team, and ESA

But here's the crazy thing: the galaxies pass through each other almost like ghosts! Cool, huh? Remember how we said there are *hundreds of billions of stars* in each and every galaxy? So how can it be that galaxies with hundreds of billions of stars, just "pass through one another" without any major collision of stars?

It's because galaxies are HUGE. Even if filled with 200 billion stars, the *volume density* of those stars is very low, simply because the volumes those galaxies occupy are so enormous. In simple words, even though there are a lot of stars, they are very, very, very far apart. To give an example of this in our home galaxy, the Milky Way, the so-called stellar density is about one solar mass per ten cubic light years. To help you picture this, even with over 200,000,000,000 stars, galaxies are mostly just empty space. As galaxies crash into each other, the stars that make up those galaxies will quietly pass one another, like ships in the night. They just won't collide, because even with four hundred billion stars flying around, there is so much empty space between then, that the chances of collision are still incredibly low.

But, I'm sure you're thinking, "I read that the odds are incredibly low, not impossible." You're a smart one, and yes, a collision *could* occur. What would happen during the collision is a complete reshaping of both galaxies by *gravity*. Even though those stars won't actually collide with one another, they will gently tug at the orbits of all their stellar neighbors as the galaxies merge, slowly and completely reshaping both galaxies participating in the crash. This process can take far more than a billion years, so the reshaping is a slow, even elegant process that turns disk-like galaxies first into beautiful irregular patterns, like those merging galaxies shown on the next page, and finally changes them into spherical stellar systems in which the orbits of stars is more like a swarm of bees than a record player.

A Hubble Space Telescope image of the Antennae Galaxies, also known as NGC 4038 and NGC 4039. These two galaxies have been crashing into one another for the past six hundred million years, resulting in this beautiful cosmic trainwreck. Credit: NASA/ESA/STScI

I need to prepare you, especially if you *actually* do have astrophobia, with the news that our galaxy, the Milky Way, will actually collide with the nearby Andromeda galaxy in about 3 billion years. (Please don't have things on your worry list that are going to happen in billions of years.) More than a billion years after the collision begins, Earth's night sky (sorry, I have to say it… that's assuming Earth, and/or humans, are still here around 3 billion years from now) will look VERY different from the calm scene you can see tonight. Andromeda will fill almost the entire sky, and in over a billion years it will reshape into a beautiful "S" shape. The Milky Way will be stretched and tugged at in a similar way, and, over the course of a little more than a billion years, it will transform from a beautiful spiral into an even more beautiful irregular galaxy. It will probably look something like this:

An artist's illustration of what the night sky on Earth might look like in about 3.5 billion years, after the Milky Way begins to merge with the Andromeda Galaxy. The shape of our galaxy will be altered forever, but actual collisions between stars will be very rare. The merger will therefore be a long, almost "gentle" process of reshaping our galaxy from a spinning disk of stars into a more spherical shape. Credit: NASA, ESA, Z. Levay and R. van der Marel (STScI), T. Hallas, and A. Mellinger

> You keep saying space is really big and you said that there are over 2 trillion galaxies. Can you help me understand how big our galaxy, the Milky Way, is with some comparison to food?

First off, I like that you think about science in terms of food. Maybe you're hungry? Or perhaps you're just hungry for knowledge! Here's an analogy that I think will help you understand why I keep saying how absolutely enormous the universe is. Picture our galaxy, the Milky Way, as a cake. Please know that the Milky Way isn't actually a cake — I bet you're thinking that Milky Way is a delicious type of candy bar — but we're going to use cake here because it has a more galaxy-like shape to serve as our model. If Earth was just one single grain of sugar inside that cake, how wide across do you think the Milky Way cake would be? First, picture one grain of sugar in your hand. Now picture all of the ingredients in a whole cake, in which that one little grain of sugar is just one tiny speck of deliciousness. How wide would this cake be that represents the scale of Earth to the Milky Way?

If Earth were the size of one grain of sugar (think about how tiny one grain of sugar would be in your hand) in a cake that is the size of the Milky Way (our galaxy), how wide across would the cake be?

My first hint is that the cake would be much larger than your entire school. It would be larger than your entire town. And not only that, the cake would be larger than the country you live in (regardless of what country!). Picture the Moon in the sky, the cake would be larger than the distance from Earth to the Moon. Ready for the answer? Take a breath because this is a little shocking… If Earth were the size of one grain of sugar, our galaxy would be a cake that is 25 million miles wide (yep… 25,000,000 miles wide! And if you think in metric that's a cake over 40,000,000 kilometers wide!). Now think about the fact that our galaxy is an average-sized galaxy and that there are over 2 trillion (2,000,000,000,000) galaxies in the universe. So, that's why I keep saying that the universe is really, really, really big! (and yes, I now want to eat some cake).

> If space is that enormous, how can you be sure that there's only one universe and in that case that there's only one me?

You're not gonna like this, but I don't know if there is only one universe and/or if there's one you. And, to make it worse, it's almost certain that, for as long as our species exists, *nobody will ever know*. It is *entirely possible that there are multiple, even an infinite number of Universes*. This would then be called a multiverse. Either possibility may be just as likely as the possibility that there is only one Universe. The problem is that this hypothesis is not remotely testable by any means we know of. It is therefore very difficult to actually advance our understanding of this theory in any real scientific way. In fact, it's more of a philosophical argument.

What is a philosophical argument?

A philosophical argument is an argument where both sides have true statements that they can make, but they are not easily resolved. Such as the classic example of what came first, the chicken or the egg? (P.S. I think it was the archaeopteryx.)

One very simple argument goes like this: if the Universe were truly *infinite*, that is, went on forever and ever and ever without end, then *every possible event would happen an infinite number of times.* There would be an infinite number of Earths, an infinite number of YOU, an infinite number of mornings in which those infinite number of *yous* had... whatever you had for breakfast this morning. We would never be *aware* of those other infinite occurrences of every possible event, however, simply because the absolute limit of our ability to observe the Universe is governed by the finite speed of light. We can only theoretically observe outward to a distance of the speed of light times the age of the Universe. While that is a *huge* volume of the Universe, if the Universe were actually infinite, it would be an *infinitesimally small* fraction of the total Universe. The multiverse, then, would simply be the same infinite universe subdivided into an infinite number of adjacent smaller universes completely unaware of their neighbors, like a patchwork quilt. Crazy, right? But kind of cool too. So how can we find out if this is true? We can't. Remember, there is no way we can test this hypothesis. We are therefore left to guess.

But hey, you never know, you may be the one to figure it out. If you ever run into a person who looks *exactly* like you, will you let me know? Now, if you happen to have an identical twin, imagine what it would be like to have an infinite number of identical twins, who aren't just your twin... they are YOU!

There could be an infinite number of universes.
Courtesy: Detlev van Ravenswaay/Science Photo Library

> My brain is kind of spinning right now. I'm going to make the questions a little less enormous and a lot less philosophical. Are there clouds in space like we have on Earth?

There are clouds almost everywhere in space. Some of these clouds are among the coldest places in the Universe, with ultra-cold "molecular gas" hovering just a few degrees above absolute zero, the lowest theoretical temperature in the Universe. It is here, in the coldest places of the cosmos, where baby stars first flicker to life, as these cold clouds collapse and become ever more dense under their own self-gravity. Gas clouds can also be extremely hot — tens of millions of degrees Fahrenheit. The largest in the Universe — giant baths of ultra-hot plasma that span the void between galaxy clusters — are the largest gravitationally relaxed structures in the Universe.

What is gravitationally relaxed?

Picture when a ball comes to rest after, say, rolling down a hill, you could call it "gravitationally relaxed." The same thing happens to giant collections of galaxies, which we call galaxy clusters.

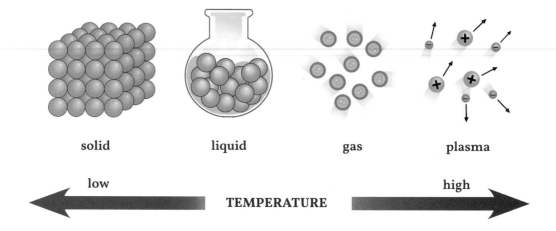

solid   liquid   gas   plasma

low   high

TEMPERATURE

You know how you thought you were making the questions less enormous. Well, these incomprehensibly giant clouds, called the intracluster medium, can be tens of millions of light years in diameter. This is incomparably large compared the clouds we see in Earth's sky. To give a sense of the size, picture a cloud that is over 2,400,000,000,000,000 (that's 2.4 *quadrillion*) times the size of Earth! Yep, we're talking about some seriously large space clouds.

This is an image of the giant galaxy at the heart of the Hercules cluster of galaxies, taken with NASA's Hubble Space Telescope, Chandra X-ray Observatory, and the National Radio Astronomy Observatory's Jansky Very Large Array. At the very center of this galaxy is a supermassive black hole belching jets of plasma (seen in blue) outward at near the speed of light. Those jets dump a lot of energy into the hot gas that the galaxy is swimming in — which you can see in pink. The one thing you can't see here is the black hole itself — that's because the scale of this image is more than 300,000 light years across, while the size of the black hole launching those giant jets is "only" about the size of our solar system. That means it's about 900 million times smaller than the size scale that this image spans. To scale, the black hole would be tinier than the tiniest pinprick you could possibly make on that image. Credit: X-ray: NASA/CXC/SAO, Optical: NASA/STScI, Radio: NSF/NRAO/VLA

Do these space clouds do anything?

Did you know that Earth's clouds are an essential part of Earth's water cycle? And that Earth's water cycle is a major part of why we have life on Earth? Well, gas clouds in space are, in many ways, the life-blood of a galaxy. They are the fuel for star formation and black hole growth, and the mechanism by which galaxies establish so-called "feedback loops," just like those seen in nature (in forests, rivers, etc.). Gas clouds also play a role in turning galaxies into incomprehensibly vast "fountains" of gas — with plumes of gas shooting out of the galaxy, only to rain back toward the galaxy center from which they came.

What's a feedback loop?

A feedback loop is when some of the output of a system cycles back in as input. Here's a simple example: The happier you are, the more hugs you give. More hugs lead to more happiness and the feedback loop continues on and on... yay for hugs (and happiness and hugs and happiness...!)

Hubble Space Telescope images of giant — and I mean giant — gas clouds called "nebulae" that are nurseries for baby stars (awww... aren't they cute?). Credit: NASA/ESA/STScI

I heard it can rain in space. Is that true?

Koh-I-Noor diamond, dimensions 3.6 cm (1.4 in) long, 3.2 cm(1.3 in) wide. Weight : 105.602 carats (21.1204 g). Compare this to the average size of an engagement ring diamond, which is 1 carat.

Yes, it rains, and not just on the edge of galaxies. You see this diamond? That's the Koh-I-Noor ("Mountain of Light"), one of the most valuable diamonds in the world. It's currently locked up in the Tower of London, where it is fastened to the front cross of the Queen Consort's crown. Hundreds of millions of dollars couldn't buy it.

It's a big deal here on Earth, but would be no big deal in other parts of the Universe. In fact, it's no big deal to Jupiter, the largest planet in our solar system. You see, it might be raining *billions* of diamonds far larger than that inside Jupiter *at this very moment.* Gas giants like Jupiter and Saturn are huge compared to Earth. You could fit more than 740 Earths inside Saturn, and more than *1,300* Earths inside Jupiter! What this means is that, though the outer layers of their gaseous atmospheres are extremely fluffy, the planets are so massive that the *density* of those atmospheres gets very high, very quickly, as you go deeper into the planet.

Jupiter, Earth size comparison

You might have heard that, when we travel underwater in submarines, the *pressure* on the submarine's hull increases as it descends to deeper depths. This is because, the deeper you go, the more water is pushing on you from all sides, increasing the force per unit area (and therefore the pressure). That's why we need very strong, very specialized submarines to reach depths where, say, the wreckage of the Titanic lies. This is also the reason why atmospheric pressure decreases when you go to higher altitudes. You might also have heard that adventurers who climb Mount Everest often need to do so with tanks of oxygen — this is because the air density at those extreme heights is very low, making physical exertion difficult and dangerous.

What's atmospheric pressure?

Atmospheric pressure is the pressure put on something that is determined by the weight of the atmosphere. For example, the atmospheric pressure decreases as you hike a mountain. And because at a higher elevation less air is pressing down on, say, a pot of water, you can boil that water at a lower temperature.

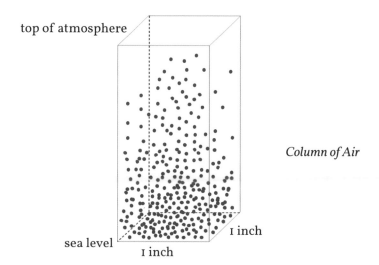

top of atmosphere

Column of Air

1 inch

sea level

1 inch

Anyway, the same thing happens in the atmospheres of gas giants, only to a far more extreme degree — just because they're so large and so massive.

In the upper layers of Jupiter and Saturn's atmospheres, violent thunderstorms are constantly raging. The lightning bolts from these storms are frequent and powerful enough to turn methane (a type of gas) into carbon-rich soot, just like the kind you find at the bottom of a fireplace or campfire. You might not think of that stuff as valuable, but if you could somehow compress that soot under extreme (and we're talking *really* extreme) pressures, it would turn into diamonds. Yep.

We think this happens in the atmospheres of Jupiter, Saturn, Neptune, and/or Uranus. It almost certainly happens in the atmospheres of faraway giant planets that exist in solar systems other than our own (we call these *exoplanets*). As that lightning-produced soot falls deeper into the gas giant's atmosphere, pressure rapidly increases. Once this rain of soot reaches extreme depths of more than 4,000 miles, that soot will be subjected to atmospheric pressures more than 3 million times greater than the atmospheric pressure you're used to on Earth. What happens then? You guessed it, that rain of soot will turn into *a rain of diamonds*. Take *that*, crown jewels.

Those incredibly large diamond raindrops will then fall at least another thirty thousand miles deeper into the planet, until conditions become so intensely hot, with such unbelievable pressures, that those diamond raindrops will turn into *liquid carbon*. They would indeed likely pool into an *ultra-hot ocean of liquid carbon*, deep within the planet.

So my guess is if this can happen on Jupiter and Saturn, it can probably happen all over the Universe (or multiverse). Right?

Now you're starting to get the way this whole enormous Universe thing works (and nice job, being fancy, using the term multiverse). We believe that, in solar systems beyond our own, there are *entire planets* that are *mostly diamond*. Yes. Planet-sized diamonds. That'd make for one heck of an engagement ring, eh?

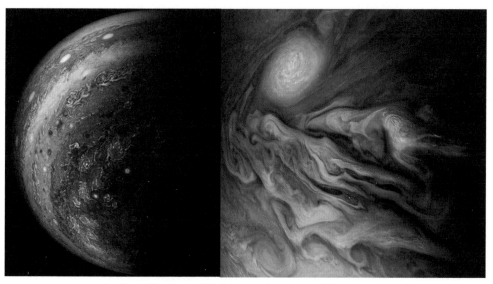

Surface of Jupiter, with close-up showing swirling gases.
Credit: NASA/SwRI/Seán Doran/Gerald Eichstädt

Could you stand on a gaseous planet?

If you think about the answer to the last question, I bet you can figure this one out. Yep, you're right. Nope, you couldn't stand on a gaseous planet. Now, that doesn't mean that a gaseous planet doesn't have a rocky, solid core — in fact, we think many *do*! *But,* in a gas giant like Jupiter, that rocky core is buried *very, very deep* within the gaseous atmosphere. And that atmosphere becomes denser and hotter as you travel deeper within it. Even if Jupiter does have a solid core you could *in theory* stand on, you *definitely* wouldn't be alive to take a stroll. The temperature near that core's surface — tens of thousands of miles deep in the atmosphere — would be a toasty *50 thousand* degrees F, and the atmospheric pressure would be 40 million times greater than at Earth's sea level. The deepest any human-made object has traveled into Jupiter's atmosphere was the *Galileo* probe, which ended its successful mission by intentionally plunging into Jupiter's atmosphere in 2003. During its final descent into the planet, it managed to transmit data to a depth of only 100 miles, recording a temperature of 300 degrees — I need to interrupt for a moment; please know that a space probe has no people in it. Okay, here we go — At that point, the rapidly increasing atmospheric pressure crushed and destroyed the probe. Its debris would have continued falling much deeper into the atmosphere, before finally being melted by the intense heat and pressure of the layers below.

The Galileo probe was released from the payload bay of the Space Shuttle Atlantis on October 18, 1989. Six years later, it arrived at Jupiter. That's a long voyage. Credit: NASA

A photo of Jupiter's moon Europa taken by the Galileo probe as it headed toward Jupiter. (Credit: NASA/JPL-Caltech/SETI Institute and we should give credit to Galileo too- and probably credit to Galileo Galilei, who Galileo, the probe, is named after!).

Who's Galileo Galilei?

Galileo Galilei lived from 1564-1642. He has been called "the father of modern science," "the father of the scientific method," "the father of observational astronomy," and "the father of modern physics." In addition to a space probe, he's had a high school, a lunar crater, a thermometer, and an airport named after him. He's awesome.

> But I could stand on the moon. Could astronauts play soccer on the moon and kick the ball back and forth? What If I kicked a soccer ball from the moon out to space, how far would it go?

So long as your team had space suits, of course you could play soccer on the moon! You've got about 1/6th of the Earth's gravity to work with, so you could kick the ball *very* far (because the gravitational acceleration is much lower, and because there's no air resistance to slow the ball during its flight), but so long as you didn't kick it too hard, it would eventually land back on the surface after flying through a slow, graceful arc.

Now, if you were an *impossibly* strong soccer player, and were somehow able to kick the ball at 1.4 *miles*

What's gravitational acceleration?

Gravitational acceleration is when an object's acceleration is caused by the force of gravity. Not that you'd ever jump off your bed onto the ground, but if you did you'd feel this.

per second upward, the ball would escape the moon's gravitational pull and leave the surface forever. But kicking a soccer ball over one mile in one second is a pretty tough goal to make.

Could a spider survive on the moon?

I hate to say this, but that poor spider is *toast*. Arachnids don't breathe like we do, but they *do* have lungs (called tracheae or book lungs) and definitely breathe the air that makes up Earth's atmosphere. The moon, I'm sorry to say, is *almost* entirely devoid of an atmosphere. Its surface is a near-complete "vacuum" — with nothing but, well, *nothingness* to breathe.

A spider and its web illuminated by the moon. That spider should not dream about traveling to the moon's surface (unless it has a space suit).

If placed on the surface of the moon, that spider would die *very* quickly. You see, the fluids in the poor spider's body would very rapidly boil off. Since spiders are so small, it's very likely that the spider would become a dried husk in a few tenths of a second. So, not only would a spider not survive, it would have a pretty dramatic, quick death.

The iconic image of astronaut Buzz Aldrin, the second human being to step on the surface of the moon (the first, Neil Armstrong, was taking the photo!). Their mission, Apollo 11, recently celebrated its 50th Anniversary. Note that, unlike our poor spider, Buzz and Neil are wearing spacesuits. Credit: NASA

This raises an interesting question, though: *why* doesn't the moon have an atmosphere? Like all matter large and small, the moon warps spacetime and creates a gravitational field strong enough that it theoretically *could* have an atmosphere. Yet, it doesn't — it's a lifeless rock, spinning in the void. What happened? Well, the moon is small enough that the *escape velocity* of anything, including gas that might form an atmosphere, is pretty low. Because the moon experiences huge variations in temperature as it passes out of the Earth's shadow and into the Sun, so-called "convective motions" in any potential atmosphere would be very high, which would lead to it being far more delicate than we would otherwise expect. Finally, the moon has no strong magnetic field to shield the atmosphere from evaporation and stripping by the solar wind (the constantly flowing streams of particles emanating from the Sun). All of these properties

What's convective motion?

Convective motion is a circular motion where warm, fast moving molecules rise and cool, slow moving molecules sink. We see this happen on Earth with convection currents in the mantle that cause our tectonic plates to move.

conspire to ensure that the moon is almost entirely devoid of anything to breathe*. Sorry, spider.

*I'll tell you a secret that most people don't know. The moon is technically surrounded by an extremely low density, puffy layer of gas called a "surface boundary exosphere." That spider is still toast — there's absolutely nothing to breathe.

Can an astronaut burp in space?

Breathing brings you to burpring, does it? Again, I like the way your mind works. The answer to this one is simple, of course! Astronauts could burp (and I'm sure many *have*) like normal inside of a pressurized spacesuit.

If they were actually exposed to the vacuum of space, burping would be even easier! This is because the pressure of gases inside your stomach would FAR exceed the ambient pressure (the pressure pushing on an object), which would be effectively zero outside of your body. That gas could very easily, and very likely would, be expelled from your body.

Now, if one's body were actually exposed to the

vacuum of space, one would have *far* bigger problems than a very bad need to burp — remember that poor spider?

Okay, I feel like I know you... you don't even have to ask. You're thinking *what would happen to a human who was exposed to the void of space?* Okay, I didn't really want to go there, but I like that you're curious. Those with astrophobia, please skip onto the next question. Trust me, you're not going to want to read this. Hmmm, how do I say this? To put it in gentle words... some *very, very* bad things would happen *very* quickly.

We have a lot in common with spiders and all other creatures that require oxygen to survive. But, there is more than that going against a human in the void of space. The absence of external pressure would cause all gases in your body, not just those in your stomach or lungs, to rapidly expand. This expansion would cause your lungs to rupture, unless you were somehow able to very quickly exhale all gas within them into space (not going to happen). Then, within seconds, nearly all of the water in the outer tissue layers of your body, like your skin, would begin to boil in the absence of pressure. I think you can imagine the rest from there, as I said... some very, very bad things would happen *very* quickly.

> What would happen to my pee in space?

Thank you for changing the topic. This is a great question with a very surprising answer: your pee would first boil, then freeze! For real, it would **boil**, then *freeze*. See, your question isn't silly, it's *totally* smart and there is a whole lot of scientific thinking that goes into the answer.

As the ambient pressure decreases, the pee's boiling point also decreases (which is why, high in the mountains, water boils at temperatures lower than 212 degrees Fahrenheit/100 degrees Celsius).

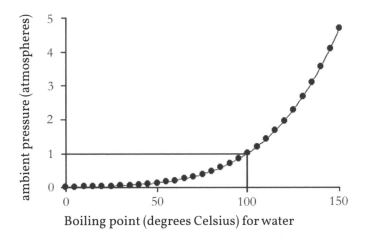

Boiling point (degrees Celsius) for water

We've actually witnessed this directly before. When astronauts ... *ahem* ... use the bathroom, the "waste" is ejected into space. On some missions, including the Apollo missions to the moon, the spacecraft design was such that exterior windows allowed views of the ports from which this waste was expelled. In the vacuum of space, where there is effectively *no* ambient pressure on the waste, the astronauts witnessed the liquid immediately boil, then *freeze*. Into ice! The waste boils because of the absence of atmospheric pressure on it. And once it boils into a vapor, those vapor particles can very rapidly cool and form ice crystals. Looking out of the command module window, the Apollo astronauts actually witnessed their waste ejection quickly form tiny ice crystals, reflecting the light of the sun. It's basically a superfine snow ... of pee.

> Space snow pee sounds cool... what temperature is space?

This is a great question with a complicated answer. Space has no temperature. I know that sounds crazy, but it's important to first understand what temperature is. Temperature is simply a measure of how fast or slowly *particles in space* are moving. The particle density of interstellar space (that is, the space between stars and solar systems) is about 1 proton per cubic cm. That is, essentially, a hard vacuum, so therefore there is no temperature. Now, the temperature *of something* in space, like a gas, is a question we can answer.

Given sufficient time, the coldest that something can get in space is about 3 K above "absolute zero" (3 kelvin), or about 455 degrees F below zero (to give a comparison, the coldest recorded temperature on a land surface in Antarctica is 128.6 degrees F below zero). What is fascinating about space is that in being a near perfect vacuum, it is also a near-perfect insulator. The temperature of, say, a lump of metal in space will be set by the balance between the energy it is absorbing, and the energy it is radiating away.

What is absolute zero?

Absolute zero is the lowest possible temperature. I'm going to say that again. Lowest. Possible. Temperature. There are people with frigophobia… a fear of becoming too cold. Shhh… Let's not tell them about absolute zero.

What's an insulator?

An insulator is a substance that does not let heat or sound easily pass through it (these keep us safe from things like electricity). The opposite of an insulator is a conductor. For example, I safely get my bagel out of the toaster oven with wooden tongs and never, ever use metal tongs. (P.S. the safest thing is to unplug the toaster oven first.)

Is there trash in space?

Nice connection between me mentioning metal in space and you thinking about trash. First off, remember "space" is huge — and so by those standards the whole Universe is huge, so no… there is very little trash in space. Low Earth orbit, however, is a very different story:

Artist's impression. Note: size of debris exaggerated as compared to the Earth. Credit: European Space Agency (ESA)

Looking at this picture, you're probably wondering where did all of this trash come from? (And I hope you read the caption and saw that the artist's scale is exaggerated). But, there is a lot of litter around Earth. No, astronauts are not littering. Or at least not intentionally littering like you might see on Earth. Part of rockets are purposely detached in space, but one of the biggest forms of space trash is satellites. Since the launch of the first-ever satellite (named *Sputnik*, launched by the Soviet Union in 1957), we humans have launched more than eight *thousand* satellites large and small. About 5,000 of these still remain in low Earth orbit, but only about 2,000 of these are actually operational and used today. That means that, in a thin shell a few hundred miles above Earth's surface, there exists a *graveyard* of dead satellites, including thousands of pieces of satellites that have long since broken apart. The US Department of Defense and NASA coordinate to keep tabs on these pieces of debris, some as small as 1 inch across. In all, there are more than 20,000 known pieces of satellite debris in

What's low Earth orbit?

Low Earth orbit is an altitude of less that 1,200 miles (2,000km) in which objects can still stay in orbit. The International Space Station stays in low Earth orbit, usually at an altitude of 217 miles (350km).

orbit. Yep, humans have led to over 20,000 pieces of space trash.

Just like pollution *on* Earth's surface, the trash in orbit is becoming an urgent problem. Satellite debris in orbit is traveling *extremely* fast relative to Earth's surface — about 17,000 miles per hour. This means that even a tiny, marble-sized piece of metallic debris can do a ton of damage to, say, the International Space Station.

The International Space Station (ISS). Credit: NASA

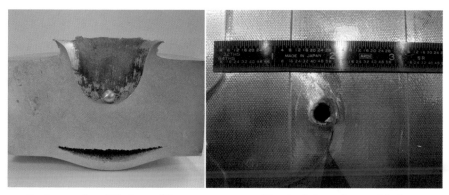

Real examples of the type of damage even a marble-sized piece of space debris can do to a spacecraft. The top image is from a space debris research project by the European Space Agency. The second image, however, is actual damage done to the Space Shuttle Endeavour during one of its missions. Credit: European Space Agency (left) and NASA (right)

Chances of collisions in low Earth orbit are still very low — often smaller than one in several hundred thousand (roughly a 0.001% chance). But it's not uncommon for spacecraft in orbit to perform a so-called "debris avoidance maneuver." The International Space Station, which has humans living aboard it, does this relatively frequently.

Junk in space is a large and growing problem that, unless something changes, will only get worse. The same, sadly, is true for the surface of our home planet. As the number of satellites in orbit grows rapidly in the coming decades, trash in space is a problem we're going to have to address, starting now (plans are already underway!).

It's even more urgent, however, to address the problem of pollution and climate change on Earth. If you want something on your worry list, climate change should absolutely be one of the top items on the list. Climate change is when the overall patterns of climate (such as temperature and the amount of rainfall) change over time. Humans are increasing the rate of climate change because of our air pollution, deforestation, overconsumption, and much more. We are impacting the well-being *of all living things on the planet*. But hope isn't lost! Your generation is rising to meet this challenge. We're all in this together, and we all must do our part to reduce our waste and carbon footprints, and forge a sustainable healthy future for our planet. Oh, and let's clean up that space junk, too.

> Can a planet be a cube?

That's actually a better transition that you may have thought. You see, basically, no. Nature is just too lazy. Yep, lazy.

You see, a sphere (that's a fancy word for a ball) is nature's preferred configuration for any self-gravitating mass. This is why, say, raindrops are little spheres, rather than cubes. In theory, through an incredibly coincidental series of very strange collisions, I guess you could briefly have a planet-sized object that was roughly the shape of a cube. But, under its own gravity, the planet's structure would pretty rapidly transform into looking much more like a sphere.

Pan, a moon of Saturn. Yes, it's actually shaped like ... what should we call it ... an overstuffed ravioli...? Incredible, right? We think the material around the moon's equator is debris from Saturn's rings that has fallen onto the surface. Credit: NASA

That picture of Pan makes me think about moons. Can moons have volcanoes?

Absolutely! The gravitational pull of Jupiter exerts extreme "tidal forces" on its closest moon, Io, which has turned it into a volcanic hellscape.

What are tidal forces?

Tidal forces are when something is pulled away and from the central mass. We see this happen on Earth with oceans and the tidal force between Earth and the Moon (and the Sun).

Io, the closest moon of Jupiter, is an incredibly violent volcano world. The lava and ash plume rises more than 150 miles above the surface of the moon. Credit: NASA (and, you guessed it, the image was taken by the Galileo spacecraft.)

So is Earth's moon kind of boring compared to other planets' moons?

I mean, no, it's not *boring*. The moon is a spectacularly fascinating environment, formed by a GIANT collision between a Mars-sized object and the Earth more than 4.5 billion years ago. The moon's structure and composition therefore encodes an archival history of the early Earth, and is our constant and beloved companion in this lonely cosmos.

BUT, having said that, I kind of have to admit... the moon is pretty boring *relative to the many other moons in our Solar system*. Liquid methane lakes on Titan. Ultra-volcanoes on Io. Chaotic rotation periods on Hyperion. A potential water ocean — *maybe*

What is a chaotic rotation period?

Chaotic rotation periods are unpredictable or irregular rotations. For example, Hyperion, one of Saturn's moons, tumbles in a completely unpredictable way. That means, if you were standing on the surface of Hyperion enjoying a sunset, you would have no idea where to expect the next sunrise. On Earth, we know almost exactly where the sun will rise every single day, because the rotation of our home planet is regular and predictable (thankfully!). Not so on Hyperion.

harboring life — below Europa's ice crust. Our moon doesn't have anything like this — except for our theoretical very dead spider. ;)

Are there the same elements in space as Earth?

Yes! The elements that make up Earth are the same as those that can be found throughout the vast reaches of the cosmos. About 4,600,000,000 years ago, the Earth formed from a gravitational instability in a giant spinning disk of cooling rock and gas whose diameter was larger than our entire solar system. That spinning disk of gas, called the solar nebula, eventually cooled and fragmented into the planets (including the Earth), asteroids, gas, and dust that orbit our Sun today.

That solar nebula was born from the remnants of previous generations of ancient stars.

Artist's impression of the solar nebula.
Credit: ESO/L. Calçada

Those stars were born from the primordial elements created in the first *seconds* of our Universe's existence, a theory we call *Big Bang Nucleosynthesis*. Stars are like great forges or factories, constantly turning light elements like hydrogen and helium into heavier elements like the iron you ate in your cereal this morning, and that flows through your veins as you read this.

If space is so big, how do scientists know all of this?

Before the mid 1920s, we had no idea that galaxies even *existed*! Astronomers had seen bright galaxies in the sky for more than a century at that point, of course, but we had no idea what they were, incorrectly referring to them as "spiral nebulae" (clouds of gas). One of the major reasons we struggled to understand

What is Big Bang nucleosynthesis?

Before the Universe, everything was contained in one very, very dense point. 13,800,000,000 years ago, that dense point experienced a big bang causing the Universe to begin through the expansion of gas and dust. "Big Bang Nucleosynthesis" is when nuclei (the central part of an atom) first formed right after that big bang.

what galaxies were was because we had no idea how to derive their distances from Earth. Then, in 1912, a brilliant astronomer at Harvard named Henrietta Swan-Leavitt discovered an astonishing, incredibly predictive relationship between the *luminosity* (brightness) of a certain type of star and the *period* of its brightness variability. If you could witness such a star vary in a "spiral nebula," you could then immediately determine its distance

Henrietta Swan-Leavitt lived from 1868 to 1921.

(because you then knew its true brightness). The "Cepheid Period-Luminosity Relation," also known as the Leavitt Law, was the tool Edwin Hubble used when he witnessed a Cepheid variable in the "spiral nebula" M31, deriving an *enormous* distance far greater than anyone could have anticipated. This was the first unambiguous piece of evidence that the spiral nebulae weren't clouds of nearby gas in our own galaxy — they were galaxies themselves, home to hundreds of billions of stars each.

What is a Cepheid variable?

A Cepheid variable is a type of star that rapidly pulsates in a way that is pretty similar to "breathing," if you will. The star's own radiation inflates its outer layers, making the star temporarily larger. As it grows in size, it begins to cool more rapidly, and so "deflates" again, starting the cycle anew. This process is so predictably regular in time, and so tightly dependent upon the brightness of the star, that it can be used as a tool by which we measure distances to extremely distant objects, like galaxies.

The Hubble Ultra Deep Field / The Hubble Space Telescope stared at an apparently empty sky for weeks, and returned this image. Nearly every single point you see in this image is a galaxy containing ~100 - 500 billion stars. Credit: NASA/ESA

That felt like a lot of words. Umm, I'm going to keep things simple. Do galaxies spin?

Yes, the vast majority of them do. This is because of *angular momentum*, one of the most important conserved quantities in nature. Galaxies grow by gravitational collapse and the collision of smaller fragments of gas and already formed stellar (super) clusters in the early Universe. Like a spinning ice skater bringing their arms in and spinning faster, those collisions conserve angular momentum, and so the merger remnant will spin. As the newly forming galaxy grows and continues to collapse under self gravity, that spin rate will increase to, again, conserve angular momentum. You can demonstrate this yourself by spinning around in a chair with your arms out.

If a balloon popped in space would it make a noise?

Hmmm... did that come from the thought of galaxies growing? Well, I'll travel this wave of curiosity with you. Sorry, that was a joke that will make sense in a minute. You're hearing sound at this moment because *matter compression waves* in the air (which are actually quite a lot like waves in the ocean) are impacting your eardrum and being registered in your brain.

The key here is that you need some sort of elastic medium for sound waves to exist and propagate. Air works perfectly for this. Water is even better. The vacuum of space? Not so much.

Basically, there is no sound in space. There's certainly no sound in a pure vacuum. If I were to answer this question absolutely correctly, I'd need many more pages to explain than there *are* actually giant sound waves in those giant clouds of gas that we spoke about earlier. In fact, we know of a black hole that is quite literally playing a musical note in the hot atmosphere of

What's elastic medium?

Elastic medium is when something can change its shape. For example, sound waves can travel through air and water because sound waves displace the air or water particles as they pass through.

plasma that pervades a distant cluster of galaxies. Cool, huh?

*Galaxy clusters — among the largest objects in the known Universe — swim in an ultra-hot, ultra-huge bath of plasma. That plasma is visible to us by the X-ray radiation it gives off, which we then image with NASA's Chandra X-ray Observatory. Here, you're seeing a Chandra image of the hot plasma in the Perseus cluster of galaxies. The image is about one million light years across. Way, way down in the center of this image is a supermassive black hole that is driving sound waves — yes, **actual** sound waves .. you can see them as ripples in the image — into the plasma. Those sound waves are in fact the lowest known musical note in the Universe — a B-flat 57 octaves below Middle C! Credit: NASA/CXC/ GSFC/S.A.Walker, et al.*

But, for our purposes, it's enough to stay that there is no sound in space. *Technically*, if you popped a balloon, the helium inside of it *would* rapidly expand into the vacuum, and there would be internal sound waves within the gas. But if you were watching this balloon pop from any sort of distance, you wouldn't hear it. Space is, basically, completely silent.

> Are there really recorded animal noises floating around in space?

Yes, you are a smart one, you find loopholes in everything! The answer to this question has entirely to do with us humans and our curiosity about whether there are other intelligent beings out there. Now that you know how enormous the Universe is, I hope you've realized that while life elsewhere in the Universe has not yet been discovered, it *is* entirely possible that there are other living organisms — which may or may not look at all like the species that are living or have lived or ever will live on Earth.

Back to your question. In 1977, NASA launched two probes, called Voyager 1 and 2. Affixed to each of their exteriors was a golden phonograph record that included carefully selected images, sounds, and music from various aspects of Earth. A committee (chaired by famous and beloved astronomer Dr. Carl Sagan) curated a collection of 115 images to encode into a gold-plated copper record to give a glimpse of what life is like on Earth. Along with these images went a few selections of music and sounds from around the world, including a greeting in dozens of languages. Over the next four decades, both probes have passed by the outer planets and have reached the *heliopause*, the boundary widely considered to be the true edge of our solar system. They have, therefore, entered interstellar space! The particle density in *interstellar space* — just a few protons per cubic centimeter — is so low that both Voyager spacecraft could remain intact for, well, *hundreds of millions to billions of years*. It is *possible* that these two tiny car-sized spacecrafts could *outlast Earth itself.*

What's interstellar space?

Interstellar space the part of space that is in between stars. (Got to love Latin roots... inter means between and stella means star. And well space, means space. Put it all together and you get... the space between stars).

Now, the chances that an advanced alien civilization finds one of the probes and decodes the record is *unbelievably* low. Not because these advanced civilizations aren't out there, but more because space is just so incredibly huge. *But*, even if the chance is *extremely small*, it's still not zero.

The gold-plated record and a picture of it being mounted onto Voyager 1. Credit: NASA/JPL

> You saying "extremely small" made me wonder... can planets shrink?

Absolutely — in fact, we think many or even *most* planets (including Earth!) are shrinking. Mercury, the planet closest to our Sun, is shrinking pretty rapidly.

This is simply because nearly all planets are *cooling*. Those in our solar system formed 4.5 billion years ago in an intensely hot, thermally unstable rotating disk of gas that was much larger than our solar system today. Planets formed in part because instabilities in this rotating disk of gas began to cool and therefore contract into planet-sized fragments.

That cooling process continues today, even 4.5 billions years on. We think the giant mountain ranges on Earth are really the result of the Earth contracting and shriveling as it cools. In fact most matter in the universe contracts as it cools (pretty cool, right?).

> You saying "matter" made me think about dark matter. What color is dark matter?

Invisible. What, you didn't know "invisible" was a color? Surely it's in your crayon box … maybe you're just not seeing it?

Sigh, okay. Dark matter's color is "gravity." Yeah, I know that's not a real color, but bear with me.

If "gravity" were a color, it'd be the most beautiful color you've ever seen. Gravity choreographs the ballet of the cosmos. It's the sculptor of the expanse. The dictator of fates. The origin of structure. It's ... uh ... the reason you spilled your milk that one time. Gravity is potentially one of the most important consequences of the laws of nature.

So, yeah. It's not a color. But it's basically *everything else.*

Dark matter has no color because it is truly "dark," in that it emits no light. It is quite unlike the normal matter that you and I are used to. We're pretty sure that the vast expanse of our Universe is permeated by unbelievably enormous filaments, or threads, of dark matter, and its only effect is manifest through the gravitational forces exerted by this dark matter on everything else. So, no --dark matter has no color because it is traditionally invisible. But its effects on normal matter are among the most important in the entire Universe. That's a lot more important than a crayon.

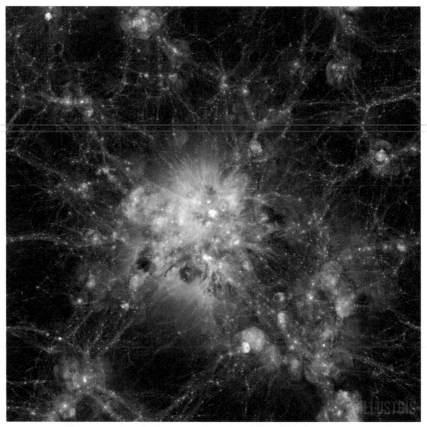

A cosmological model for the Universe, consisting mostly of dark matter and so-called "dark energy." Credit: Illustris Simulation

Could I ever travel at the speed of light?

Not if you'd like to avoid becoming INFINITELY MASSIVE. You see, mass is the same thing as energy (thanks, Einstein, for figuring that out). Because of this, as you start accelerating toward the speed of light, your mass starts to increase. We think the speed of light is a sort of universal speed limit, because an object with any so-called "nonzero rest mass" could never actually reach the speed of light. The faster you go, the heavier you get. The only thing that can travel at the universal speed limit of 186,282 miles per second is something with zero rest mass — a particle we call a photon. That spaceship you've been dreaming up? I don't care how fancy its engines are, the spacecraft has *some* mass. And because of that, it can never actually reach the speed of light.

What is nonzero rest mass?

A nonzero rest mass is an object that can't reach the speed of light. No matter how fast you may be at running, my friend, you are an object with nonzero rest mass.

What's a photon?

A photon is one particle of light. Here's a classic physics joke. A photon walks into a hotel. They ask if he has any luggage. The photon says, "No, of course not. I'm traveling light." (Before I get a follow up question… Please note: photons don't actually speak, they are particles of light).

> I can't travel at the speed of light and the Milky Way would be a 25 million mile wide cake in your earlier answer, so my guess is that means I probably won't get to explore this universe that we've talked so much about?

I do want to remind you that you and Earth and everything you see are a part of this universe. Also, telescopes, small and large, are a great way to explore the universe from the comfort of your own planet. But, my guess is that you are picturing yourself in a high tech spaceship. I will start by saying who knows what will exist in the future, but the fastest spacecraft ever created by the human species is *New Horizons*, which took a decade to travel to Pluto. Traveling at this speed, it would take 78,000 years just to reach *Alpha Proxima*, the nearest star, 4.2 light years from Earth. Our galaxy, consisting of hundreds of billions of stars in a slowly rotating disk, spans at least 30 kiloparsecs in diameter, and several kiloparsecs in thickness. It would take this craft, traveling at 36,000 mph, 607 million years to travel just 10 kpc, which is just about the smallest possible distance one could travel to truly "leave" the galaxy. So, if you're trying to physically leave the Milky Way galaxy within one human lifespan, at this moment in time, with current Earthling technology, that is not possible.

An image of the spiral galaxy NGC 1232. We can't take a similar picture of our home galaxy, the Milky Way, because we live inside it. But if we could fly outside of our galaxy and take such an image, we think it'd look a lot like NGC 1232 does.
Credit: ESO

Last, but not least, you said "at this moment in time." I've heard looking into space is like looking back in time. Is that true?

YES!

In fact, you're looking back in time *as you read these words*. You have indeed *never* witnessed the present time in your entire life. You are *always* looking back in time.

This is because your eyes see by collecting light. Light, in turn, is made of that thing we talked about earlier called *photons*. And while those photons travel quickly (186,000 miles per second), they don't travel infinitely quickly. This means that they take *time* to travel from their source (the thing you're seeing) to their destination (your eyeballs). If you're looking at your friend standing one foot away from you, you're looking at them as they were approximately one nanosecond (one billionth of a second) in the past.

You're time traveling! If they step another foot away from you, you're looking at them even deeper into the past — *two* nanoseconds.

And so, if you're looking at a star 76 light years away, your eyes are collecting photons that were born in that star while World War II was still raging here on Earth. In the intervening 76 years, those photons traveled 446,800,000,000,000 miles to land upon your eyeballs.

If you're looking at a galaxy in the Virgo cluster of galaxies, your eyes are collecting photons that departed those galaxies while dinosaurs still roamed the Earth (over 65,000,000 years ago!).

So, yes. You're looking at historical events *right now.*

To take this idea to an extreme: in *theory*, if you had a *perfect* telescope that could resolve impossibly small spatial scales, and if you boarded a (non-existent) science fiction spacecraft that could travel much faster than the speed of light (which we don't think is possible), then you could, say, travel 2,063 light years away, turn your (impossibly perfect) telescope back toward Earth, and watch the assassination of Julius Caesar at the Theater of Pompey in 44 BC. You could travel 65 million light years away and watch the extinction of the dinosaurs. You could travel 4.5 billion light years away and watch the formation of Earth itself.

This thought experiment isn't practically possible, of course, but everything above is *technically* an entirely true statement. Time travel isn't science fiction. It is an everyday reality. Looking through space is *identical* to looking through time. Pretty cool, huh?

Let's end with one very cool photograph of an actual black hole. You started your questions by asking what black holes eat for dinner. I hope you've learned the answer, plus a whole lot more!

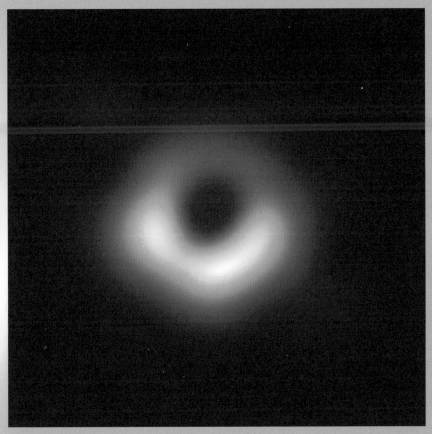

The Event Horizon Telescope (EHT) — a planet-scale array of eight ground-based radio telescopes forged through international collaboration — was designed to capture images of a black hole. In coordinated press conferences across the globe, EHT researchers revealed that they succeeded, unveiling the first direct visual evidence of the supermassive black hole in the centre of Messier 87 and its shadow. Credit: Event Horizon Telescope Collaboration

That was fun taking a journey through space and in many ways a journey through your curiosity. You've got a great way of thinking! Keep wondering. Keep asking questions. Keep seeking out the answers. And, someday you may be the one making new discoveries that change all of our understanding of the Universe! (Please feel no pressure here. Plus, the thing about science is whatever is figured out, will probably be better understood by someone else in the future.) In the meantime, let's be grateful for our planet and the endless possibilities of our *really, really* big universe.

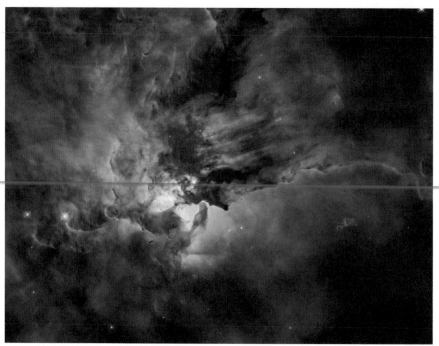

The Lagoon Nebula. Credit: ESA/Hubble

ACKNOWLEDGMENTS

Thank you to the staff at Tumblehome for believing in this project! Penny's Noyce's feedback on earlier versions helped us reshape our vision and led to a far more palatable approach (we had to make a food joke there because earlier versions, sadly, included no mention of dinner and didn't include any humor). And a huge thank you to Yu-Yi Ling for her artistic vision and endless effort on the book's layout and design!

Thank you to Andrew McCullough for being the connection that brought Grant and Katie together (a best friend to one and a husband to another). Thank you to Aurea, Iris, and Adelaide for inspiring us (and for being good sleepers, so we could work on this project)!

Thank you to Katie's students for brainstorming questions about space that helped inspire many of the questions in this book. Thank you to a few students in particular: Jenna R. read an early version of the manuscript and gave helpful feedback. And, Thomas H. and Quinn H. were the creators of the feedback loop idea of hugs and happiness that they shared in class during a lesson on feedback loops given by Katie's co-teacher, Mat Holmes.

Thank you to NASA (and those who led to, and supported, NASA's technological advances) for providing many of the public domain images that are used throughout this book.

ABOUT THE AUTHORS

Dr. Grant Tremblay is an Astrophysicist at the Center for Astrophysics — Harvard & Smithsonian. He was previously a NASA Einstein Fellow at Yale University, a Fellow at the European Southern Observatory (ESO), and a Fellow Astronomer at ESO's Very Large Telescope in Chile. His Doctoral Thesis work was conducted at the Space Telescope Science Institute (operations center for the *Hubble Space Telescope*), the Johns Hopkins University, and the Rochester Institute of Technology. He is heavily involved in the development of future NASA space missions, and is the Deputy Lead for the *Lynx X-ray Observatory* project at the Smithsonian, a Flagship NASA mission under consideration for launch in the late 2030s. He is an author on more than seventy scientific publications, as well as Light From the Void, (from Smithsonian Books) which celebrates two decades of discovery with the *Chandra X-ray Observatory*. He is also a regular cast member on the *Discovery* and *Science* Channel's award-winning documentary series *How the Universe Works* and *Space's Deepest Secrets*, as well as the host of a forthcoming *Smithsonian Channel* miniseries on black holes. For more information, please visit www.granttremblay.com.

photo ty Brendan Bullock

Katie Coppens lives in Maine with her husband and two children. She is an award-winning teacher who currently teaches sixth grade science and English at Falmouth Middle School. She has a range of experience from teaching self-contained third grade to teaching high school biology and English in Tanzania. Katie's goal is to write books that encourage kids to ask questions and have fun while learning. Katie has multiple publications, including a teacher's guide for the National Science Teaching Association entitled *Creative Writing in Science: Activities That Inspire, Geology is a Piece of Cake, Geometry is as Easy as Pie*, and *The Acadia Files* chapter book series. Katie also writes a column for NSTA's *Science Scope* magazine called "Interdisciplinary Ideas." Go to www.katiecoppens.com for more information on her publications.

IMAGE CREDITS